Biography®

Visionaries *of the* 20th Century

Biography ®

Desk Diary 2000

Visionaries *of the* 20th Century

Text by Paula Rice Jackson

A&E ®

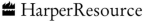

HarperResource

An Imprint of HarperCollinsPublishers

Dates for the seasons and phases of the moon are given in Eastern
Standard Time and Eastern Daylight Savings Time.

Edited by Lois Brown
Designed by Christina Bliss, Staten Island

ISBN 0-06-270241-6

Painting is just another way of keeping a diary. —PABLO PICASSO

No man can sit down and withhold his hands from the warfare against wrong and get peace from his acquiescence. —WOODROW WILSON

It is in the knowledge of the genuine conditions of our lives that we must draw our strength to live and our reasons for living. —SIMONE DE BEAUVOIR

The responsibility of great states is to serve and not to dominate the world. —HARRY S. TRUMAN

There is a vitality, a life force, an energy, a quickening, that is translated through you into action, and because there is only one of you in all time, this expression is unique. —MARTHA GRAHAM

Living is a form of not knowing what next or how. The moment you know how, you begin to die a little. The artist never entirely knows. We guess. We may be wrong, but we take leap after leap in the dark. —AGNES DEMILLE

No one can make you feel inferior without your consent. —ELEANOR ROOSEVELT

Fashion is made to become unfashionable. —COCO CHANEL

What we play is life. —LOUIS ARMSTRONG

Imagination is more important than knowledge. —ALBERT EINSTEIN

In almost any society, I think, the quality of the nonconformists is likely to be just as good as and no better than that of the conformists. —MARGARET MEAD

When you love you wish to do things for. You wish to sacrifice for. You wish to serve. —ERNEST HEMINGWAY, A FAREWELL TO ARMS

The problems of victory are more agreeable than those of defeat, but they are no less difficult. —WINSTON CHURCHILL

It is easy enough to be friendly to one's friends. But to befriend the one who regards himself as your enemy is the quintessence of true religion. The other is mere business. —MOHANDAS GANDHI

Ask not what your country can do for you, but, rather, what you can do for your country. —JOHN F. KENNEDY

The only thing we have to fear is fear itself—nameless, unreasoning, unjustified terror which paralyzes needed efforts to convert retreat into advance. —FRANKLIN D. ROOSEVELT

Rattling the bones is not architecture. Less is only more where more is no good. —FRANK LLOYD WRIGHT

Say the "Secret Word" and win a hundred dollars. —GROUCHO MARX

December ~ January

27 MON

28 TUES

29 WED

30 THURS

31 FRI

1 SAT • New Year's Day

2 SUN

SIMONE DE BEAUVOIR
Born 1908 in Paris, France; d. 1986

December 1999

S	M	T	W	T	F	S
			1	2	3	4
5	6	7	8	9	10	11
12	13	14	15	16	17	18
19	20	21	22	23	24	25
26	27	28	29	30	31	

January 2000

S	M	T	W	T	F	S
						1
2	3	4	5	6	7	8
9	10	11	12	13	14	15
16	17	18	19	20	21	22
23	24	25	26	27	28	29
30	31					

A&E

The Second Sex, published in 1949 by French existentialist writer Simone de Beauvoir, startled world thought with its unflinching analysis of unconscious mechanisms of culture that impaired women's social and economic progress. As a young woman de Beauvoir rebelled against a provincial upbringing and studied philosophy at the Sorbonne with Jean-Paul Sartre, with whom she had a notorious affair. They remained lifelong companions until his death in 1980. Her own works provide existentialism with an essentially feminine sensibility, and her masterpiece, *The Mandarins* (1954), was awarded the Prix Goncourt.

Simone de Beauvoir on vacation in Rome with Jean Paul Sartre, 1967. AP/Wide World Photos

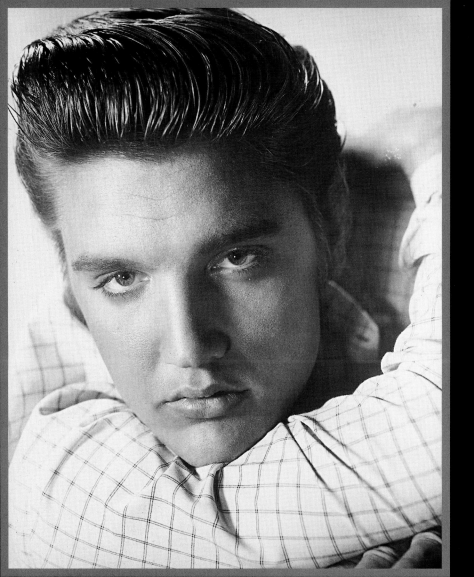

Church choirs have served as the training ground for some of America's most famous popular singers, and the Church of the Assembly of God is where Elvis Presley got his training. In 1956 he had his first nationwide record hit, "Heartbreak Hotel," and appeared on television's Ed Sullivan Show, where the cameras were never permitted to shoot below his waist. He made 33 films, served in Germany while in the army, and scored his last chart-topping single in 1969. He adopted a Las Vegas-style showmanship that earned him the sobriquet "The King," which he kept until his sad, early death, brought about by his flamboyant lifestyle.

Photos used by permission of Elvis Presley Enterprises, Inc.

MON **3**

ELVIS AARON
PRESLEY
Born in 1935 in
Tupelo, Miss.; d. 1977

TUES **4**

WED **5**

New Moon • THURS **6**

FRI **7**

Elvis Presley's Birthday, 1935 • SAT **8**

Simone de Beauvoir's Birthday, 1908 • SUN **9**

A&E

10 MON

11 TUES

12 WED

CHRISTIAN DIOR
Born in 1905 in Granville, France; d. 1957

13 THURS

14 FRI • 1st Quarter Moon

15 SAT

16 SUN

January

S	M	T	W	T	F	S
						1
2	3	4	5	6	7	8
9	10	11	12	13	14	15
16	17	18	19	20	21	22
23	24	25	26	27	28	29
30	31					

February

S	M	T	W	T	F	S
		1	2	3	4	5
6	7	8	9	10	11	12
13	14	15	16	17	18	19
20	21	22	23	24	25	26
27	28	29				

$\mathcal{C}$reator of the so-called New Look in 1947, Christian Dior brought back a sense of glamour and seductiveness to World-War-II-weary women worldwide who had scrimped and sacrificed their sense of fashion identity for so many years. The New Look was more an attitude of beauty and grace toward femininity than it was a hemline (long, waltz-length, and full). Dior began designing clothes in 1935, trained with Robert Piguet, founded his own house in 1945, and ascended the world stage two years later with his understanding of what women wanted and needed. Dior ruled fashion, not merely as a sovereign, but as an evolving creative force.

Photos courtesy Christian Dior Couturé. Schuman ballgown 1950, photo by Louise Dahl Wolfe, © 1989 Collection Center for Creative Photography, Arizona Board of Regents, University of Arizona

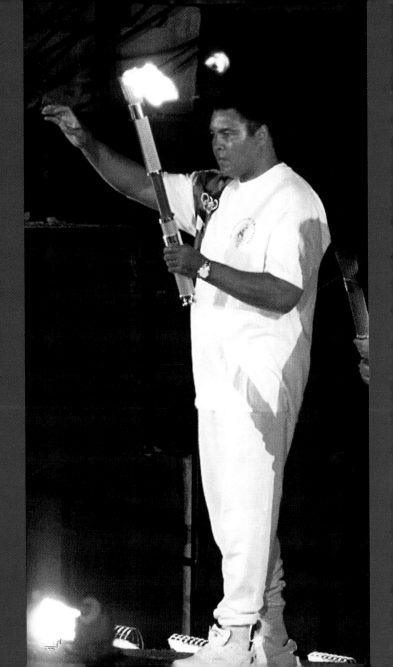

𝒥n a career that celebrated 56 wins and 37 knockout punches, boxer Muhammad Ali has become the poet of the art. Winning the world heavyweight championship with his unexpected defeat of Sonny Liston in 1964, the boxer formerly known as Cassius Clay declared his victory an "act of God," became a Muslim, changed his name, defended his title successfully for two years, announced himself a pacifist according to Muslim strictures, and was stripped of his title in 1967. His rights as a conscientious objector were unanimously upheld by the U.S. Supreme Court, but ten years were to pass before he regained his title by knocking out George Foreman in 1974. Ali raised the public image of boxing to a new level of purpose, entertainment, and wealth, but it is his personal qualities of determined truth, persistence, and kindness that have earned him the admiration of fans worldwide. Having contributed more toward humanity than perhaps any other athlete, Ali has raised millions of dollars for charitable causes, crossed continents to deliver food and medical supplies to needy children, journeyed to Iraq to secure the release of U.S. hostages, and traveled across the globe urging people to embrace tolerance and understanding. Cited as a United Nations Messenger of Peace by the secretary-general of the U.N., Ali was honored with Amnesty International's Lifetime Achievement Award in 1998.

Muhammad Ali at the opening ceremonies of the Atlanta Summer Olympics, 1996. AP/Wide World Photos

Martin Luther King, Jr. Day • Muhammad Ali's Birthday, 1942 • MON **17**

MUHAMMAD ALI
Born in 1942 in
Louisville, Ky.

TUES **18**

WED **19**

Full Moon • THURS **20**

Christian Dior's Birthday, 1905 • FRI **21**

D.W. Griffith's Birthday, 1875 • SAT **22**

SUN **23**

January

S	M	T	W	T	F	S
						1
2	3	4	5	6	7	8
9	10	11	12	13	14	15
16	17	18	19	20	21	22
23	24	25	26	27	28	29
30	31					

February

S	M	T	W	T	F	S
		1	2	3	4	5
6	7	8	9	10	11	12
13	14	15	16	17	18	19
20	21	22	23	24	25	26
27	28	29				

A&E

24 MON

25 TUES

26 WED

27 THURS

28 FRI • Last Quarter Moon

29 SAT

30 SUN • Franklin D. Roosevelt's Birthday, 1882

DAVID LEWELYN
WARK GRIFFITH
Born in 1875 in La
Grange, Ky.; d. 1948

January

S	M	T	W	T	F	S
						1
2	3	4	5	6	7	8
9	10	11	12	13	14	15
16	17	18	19	20	21	22
23	24	25	26	27	28	29
30	31					

February

S	M	T	W	T	F	S
		1	2	3	4	5
6	7	8	9	10	11	12
13	14	15	16	17	18	19
20	21	22	23	24	25	26
27	28	29				

A&E

In the early 20th century, Biograph Pictures was one of the few solvent film companies in the fledgling industry of moviemaking. D. W. Griffith learned the technical and directorial arts of this craft while general director at the studio, a period which culminated in what many critics and historians agree was America's first "important" film epic, *Birth of a Nation*, produced by Reliance-Majestic. Along with Charlie Chaplin, Griffith was one of the founders of United Artists in 1919. He received special Academy Award recognition in 1935 for his contribution to the evolution of an art form and an industry.

Elected to baseball's Hall of Fame in 1962, Jackie Robinson became the first African-American professional player in the modern-era major leagues to cross the so-called color barrier when he was brought up as infielder for the Brooklyn Dodgers in 1947. He led the Dodgers to six National League championships and the club's first World Series victory in 1955. He was named the National League's Most Valuable Player in 1949. After retiring from baseball, he was an active spokesperson for civil rights, having endured and prevailed over the discrimination he faced in his early, progressive years.

Ebbetts Field, Brooklyn, May 29, 1947, Robinson at first base.™/©1998 Rachel Robinson under license authorized by CMG Worldwide Inc., Indianapolis, IN. AP/Wide World Photos

Jackie Robinson's Birthday, 1919 • MON **31**

JACK ROOSEVELT ROBINSON
Born in 1919 in Cairo, Ga.; d. 1972

TUES *1*

WED *2*

THURS *3*

S	M	T	W	T	F	S
						1
2	3	4	5	6	7	8
9	10	11	12	13	14	15
16	17	18	19	20	21	22
23	24	25	26	27	28	29
30	31					

Ida Lupino's Birthday, 1918 • FRI *4*

New Moon • SAT *5*

February

S	M	T	W	T	F	S
		1	2	3	4	5
6	7	8	9	10	11	12
13	14	15	16	17	18	19
20	21	22	23	24	25	26
27	28	29				

SUN *6*

February

7 MON

8 TUES

9 WED

10 THURS

11 FRI

12 SAT • Lincoln's Birthday • 1st Quarter Moon

13 SUN

FRANKLIN
DELANO
ROOSEVELT
Born in 1882 in Hyde
Park, NY; d. 1945

February

S	M	T	W	T	F	S
		1	2	3	4	5
6	7	8	9	10	11	12
13	14	15	16	17	18	19
20	21	22	23	24	25	26
27	28	29				

March

S	M	T	W	T	F	S
		1	2	3	4
5	6	7	8	9	10	11
12	13	14	15	16	17	18
19	20	21	22	23	24	25
26	27	28	29	30	31	

A&E

America's patrician 32nd president Franklin Delano Roosevelt took office during the years of the deepening Great Depression. His New Deal ushered in social and economic perspectives that set the pattern for the modern liberal Democratic Party. The Tennessee Valley Authority, Social Security, the Works Progress Administration, and the Securities and Exchange Commission were created during the first of the three full terms that he served. He steadfastly held to a neutralist policy in World War II, but began supplying the Allies in 1940 and formally entered the United States into the war after the bombing of Pearl Harbor in 1941.Though Roosevelt came as close to being a "dictator" as America has ever had, historians agree that as a force for good, his results were unparalleled.

Photos courtesy the Franklin D. Roosevelt Library

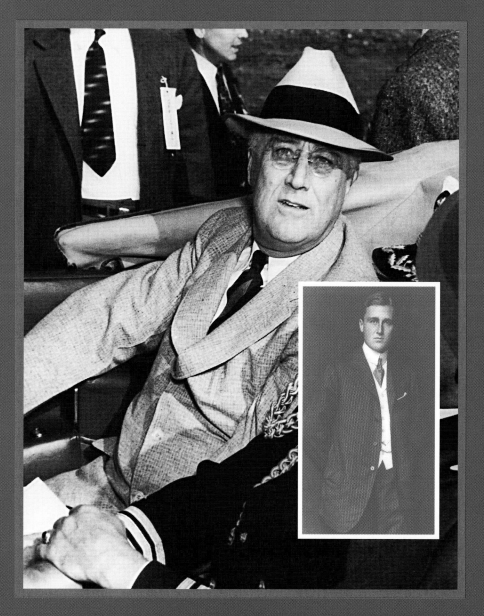

The descendant of a distinguished British theatrical family, actress Ida Lupino began her film career in England but transplanted herself to Hollywood, where she found herself slotted into a "new" category of film star: the tough woman, as seen in *Beware My Lovely* (1952). The image must have appealed to her at a deeper level; she began to prefer writing, directing, and producing movies and made-for-television films to acting. She is credited with being one of the first stars to turn director/producer, and as a woman she paved the way for future actresses who dared to change their minds and produce in a male-dominated world.

OPPOSITE: Ida Lupino working on the suspense drama The Difference, *which she directed. Photos ™/© 1998 Ida Lupino under license authorized by CMG Worldwide Inc., Indianapolis, IN. Publicity photo of Ida Lupino © 1941 Warner Bros., a division of Time Warner Entertainment Co., L.P. Photos Culver Pictures, Inc.*

February

Valentine's Day • MON *14*

IDA LUPINO
Born in 1918 in
London, England;
d. 1995

Susan B. Anthony's Birthday, 1820 • TUES *15*

WED *16*

THURS *17*

FRI *18*

Full Moon • SAT *19*

SUN *20*

February

S	M	T	W	T	F	S
		1	2	3	4	5
6	7	8	9	10	11	12
13	14	15	16	17	18	19
20	21	22	23	24	25	26
27	28	29				

March

S	M	T	W	T	F	S
			1	2	3	4
5	6	7	8	9	10	11
12	13	14	15	16	17	18
19	20	21	22	23	24	25
26	27	28	29	30	31	

21 MON • Presidents' Day

22 TUES • Washington's Birthday

DAVID SARNOFF
Born in 1891 in
Minsk, Russia; d. 1971

23 WED

24 THURS

25 FRI

February

S	M	T	W	T	F	S
		1	2	3	4	5
6	7	8	9	10	11	12
13	14	15	16	17	18	19
20	21	22	23	24	25	26
27	28	29				

26 SAT • Last Quarter Moon

March

S	M	T	W	T	F	S
			1	2	3	4
5	6	7	8	9	10	11
12	13	14	15	16	17	18
19	20	21	22	23	24	25
26	27	28	29	30	31	

27 SUN • David Sarnoff's Birthday, 1891

_S_peaking no English when he arrived in New York City at the age of nine, David Sarnoff learned the language in the environs of Hell's Kitchen and spent the rest of his life improving communications among people technologically. At age 15, he was hired as an office boy by American Marconi Wireless; by 16 he was managing one of Marconi's four land-based stations; and in 1912, he picked up the first distress messages from the sinking _Titanic_. The Radio Corporation of America (RCA), successor to Marconi, offered Sarnoff the forum his genius required. Seeing the common sense in radio as a household utility, he set up a broadcasting system that he later expanded to include television. He pursued his vision relentlessly and became RCA's third president in 1930 and later its chairman. He organized the National Broadcasting Company (NBC) and from the 30s to the 50s made RCA the center for development of the electronic black-and-white and compatible color TV systems used today.

Young Sarnoff on duty at the Marconi Nantucket Island station, c. 1908. Photos RCA, courtesy the David Sarnoff Collection, Inc., Princeton, NJ

As the cofounder of the National Woman Suffrage Association in 1869 with Elizabeth Cady Stanton, Susan B. Anthony is credited with defining the issues of "women's rights," a subject almost unthinkable in that age and time. She constantly spoke out against injustices concerning women's property and rights to their children, equal pay, and access to education, but concentrated most of her energies during her final decades to seeking a constitutional amendment allowing women to vote. She lived to see the feminist movement advance toward respectability and political importance.

Photos courtesy Susan B. Anthony House, 17 Madison St., Rochester, NY, who are raising funds for restoration. Coin © Lynton Gardiner Photography, NY

MON **28**

SUSAN B. ANTHONY
Born 1820 in Adams, Mass., of Quaker parentage; d. 1906

TUES **29**

WED **1**

THURS **2**

February

S	M	T	W	T	F	S
		1	2	3	4	5
6	7	8	9	10	11	12
13	14	15	16	17	18	19
20	21	22	23	24	25	26
27	28	29				

FRI **3**

March

S	M	T	W	T	F	S
			1	2	3	4
5	6	7	8	9	10	11
12	13	14	15	16	17	18
19	20	21	22	23	24	25
26	27	28	29	30	31	

SAT **4**

SUN **5**

6 MON • New Moon

7 TUES

8 WED

9 THURS

10 FRI • Clare Boothe Luce's Birthday, 1903

11 SAT

12 SUN

CLARE BOOTHE LUCE
Born in 1903 in New York City; d. 1987

March

S	M	T	W	T	F	S
			1	2	3	4
5	6	7	8	9	10	11
12	13	14	15	16	17	18
19	20	21	22	23	24	25
26	27	28	29	30	31	

April

S	M	T	W	T	F	S
						1
2	3	4	5	6	7	8
9	10	11	12	13	14	15
16	17	18	19	20	21	22
23	24	25	26	27	28	29
30						

Clare Boothe Luce could be described as one of the nation's first superwomen. Journalist, editor, playwright, politician, and ambassador—she did it all. Her hit Broadway play *The Women* (1936) is still being revived and analyzed; her marriage to Henry Luce, the founder and owner of *Time* magazine, was a major alliance; and her position as a witty and acerbic arbiter of popular taste still has its effect. She helped define the arena in which ambitious, talented, determined women could make a professional contribution. She served as the American ambassador to Italy during the Eisenhower administration (1953–1956).

AP/Wide World Photos

𝓘n 1928 Steamboat Willie was the first name given to the cartoon creature in the first sound cartoon ever made. He is now known as Mickey Mouse. Walt Disney was a movie animator, a producer, and a showman who later came to be one of America's most brilliant businessmen. His full-length animated features constitute a popular element of American culture equally as important as any historical artifact. In 1955 Disneyland opened as a theme park dedicated to characters that have since become a part of the American landscape.

Photos © Disney Enterprises, Inc.

1st Quarter Moon • MON **13**

E∂z

WALTER ELIAS DISNEY
Born in 1901 in
Chicago, Ill.; d. 1966

Albert Einstein's Birthday, 1879 • TUES **14**

μ

WED **15**

THURS **16**

March

S	M	T	W	T	F	S
			1	2	3	4
5	6	7	8	9	10	11
12	13	14	15	16	17	18
19	20	21	22	23	24	25
26	27	28	29	30	31	

St. Patrick's Day • FRI **17**

April

S	M	T	W	T	F	S
						1
2	3	4	5	6	7	8
9	10	11	12	13	14	15
16	17	18	19	20	21	22
23	24	25	26	27	28	29
30						

SAT **18**

Full Moon • SUN **19**

20 MON • Spring begins

Ez

21 TUES

ALBERT EINSTEIN
Born 1879 in Ulm,
Germany; d. 1955

22 WED

M

23 THURS

24 FRI

March

S	M	T	W	T	F	S
			1	2	3	4
5	6	7	8	9	10	11
12	13	14	15	16	17	18
19	20	21	22	23	24	25
26	27	28	29	30	31	

25 SAT

April

S	M	T	W	T	F	S
						1
2	3	4	5	6	7	8
9	10	11	12	13	14	15
16	17	18	19	20	21	22
23	24	25	26	27	28	29
30						

26 SUN

$\mathcal{A}$lbert Einstein's general theory of relativity effectively displaced Newtonian mechanics as the cornerstone of physics and opened world thought to a new concept of time and space. As the Nazis came to power in Germany he was deprived of his property and his citizenship and emigrated to the United States. Alarmed by Nazi expansion, he appealed to President Roosevelt to begin work on an atomic bomb. Though he never worked on that project, later known as the Manhattan Project, much of his knowledge of the behavior of atoms was applied to it. Einstein was also an accomplished violinist and a Zionist. One of his most controversial books, *Why War?*, was written with Sigmund Freud.

$\mathcal{S}$am Walton was a master at understanding customers and motivating people, and he appreciated the importance of providing small-town and rural customers a wide assortment of products,with a smile. He was a successful operator of a chain of five-and-dime stores based in Arkansas in the 1940s and 50s. In 1962, he founded Wal-Mart, which had a wildly successful formula of offering brand-name goods at low prices at convenient locations. By 1998, Wal-Mart operated 3,600 stores and clubs in nine countries and, on average, was opening or acquiring almost one new unit every business day. Annual sales of the company that same year exceeded $130 billion, making it by far the largest retailer in the world.

WAL★MART
SUPERCENT
PHARMACY

Sam M. Walton

Photos courtesy Walton Enterprises and Wal-Mart Stores, Inc.

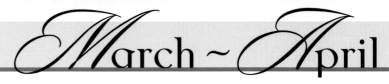

Last Quarter Moon • MON **27**

ER

SAMUEL MOORE WALTON
Born in 1918 in Kingfisher, Okla.; d. 1992

TUES **28**

ER

Samuel M. Walton's Birthday, 1918 • WED **29**

 # ER

THURS **30**

March

S	M	T	W	T	F	S
			1	2	3	4
5	6	7	8	9	10	11
12	13	14	15	16	17	18
19	20	21	22	23	24	25
26	27	28	29	30	31	

FRI **31**

April

S	M	T	W	T	F	S
						1
2	3	4	5	6	7	8
9	10	11	12	13	14	15
16	17	18	19	20	21	22
23	24	25	26	27	28	29
30						

SAT **1**

Daylight Savings Time begins • SUN **2**

3   MON

4   TUES • New Moon

**BETTY FORD
(Elizabeth
Anne Bloomer)**
Born in Chicago, 1918

5   WED

6   THURS

April

S	M	T	W	T	F	S
						1
2	3	4	5	6	7	8
9	10	11	12	13	14	15
16	17	18	19	20	21	22
23	24	25	26	27	28	29
30						

7   FRI

8   SAT • Betty Ford's Birthday, 1918

May

S	M	T	W	T	F	S
	1	2	3	4	5	6
7	8	9	10	11	12	13
14	15	16	17	18	19	20
21	22	23	24	25	26	27
28	29	30	31			

9   SUN

As wife of President Gerald Ford and as First Lady of the nation, Betty Ford fearlessly spoke out on women's issues, including her own bout with breast cancer. But later her problems with alcohol and prescription drugs almost consumed her. These were afflictions that people were reluctant to speak about openly. After Ford's dramatic and painful recovery from chemical dependency, she courageously went before the public to tell her story as living proof that one can recover. She went on to establish the Betty Ford Center in California, one of the most outstanding drug dependency treatment facilities in the nation.

Gerald and Betty Ford on their wedding day in 1948. Photos courtesy Gerald R. Ford Library

The sons of the bishop of the United Brethren Church of Dayton, Ohio, Wilbur and Orville Wright both showed an unusual facility for mechanics from early childhood. The brothers became recognized pioneers of aviation, having built their first glider, a biplane with wings that could be twisted mechanically, in 1899. On December 17, 1903, both brothers flew independently, when Orville piloted a flight of 12 seconds and 120 feet; Wilbur flew later in the day, staying aloft for 59 seconds and covering 852 feet. By 1906 they were awarded a patent for their powered aircraft, and in 1909 the American Wright Company began to manufacture planes and to train pilots for the U.S. War Department. Wilbur, a bachelor (as was his brother), died of typhoid in 1912. Orville, who lived until 1948, remained active in aeronautic research.

Photos The Smithsonian Institution, National Air and Space Museum

MON 10

WILBUR WRIGHT
Born in 1867 in
Millville, Ind.; d. 1912

1st Quarter Moon • TUES 11

ORVILLE WRIGHT
Born 1871 in Dayton,
Ohio; d. 1948

WED 12

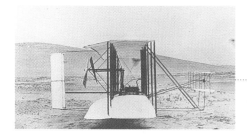

THURS 13

April

S	M	T	W	T	F	S
						1
2	3	4	5	6	7	8
9	10	11	12	13	14	15
16	17	18	19	20	21	22
23	24	25	26	27	28	29
30						

FRI 14

May

S	M	T	W	T	F	S
	1	2	3	4	5	6
7	8	9	10	11	12	13
14	15	16	17	18	19	20
21	22	23	24	25	26	27
28	29	30	31			

SAT 15

Wilbur Wright's Birthday, 1867 • SUN 16

A&E

17 MON

18 TUES • Full Moon

**GOLDA MEIR
(born Mabovitch)**
Born in 1898 in Kiev,
Ukraine; d. 1978

19 WED

20 THURS • Passover begins

April

S	M	T	W	T	F	S
						1
2	3	4	5	6	7	8
9	10	11	12	13	14	15
16	17	18	19	20	21	22
23	24	25	26	27	28	29
30						

21 FRI • Good Friday

22 SAT

May

S	M	T	W	T	F	S
	1	2	3	4	5	6
7	8	9	10	11	12	13
14	15	16	17	18	19	20
21	22	23	24	25	26	27
28	29	30	31			

23 SUN • Easter

Her family came to the United States in 1906; later, Golda Meir became a teacher and an active Zionist in Milwaukee. She and her husband emigrated to Palestine in 1921, where she worked as a labor activist. She was elected to the Israeli parliament in 1949 and held portfolios in both labor and foreign affairs. She was elected Israel's fourth prime minister, a post she held from 1969 to 1974, benefiting by Israel's triumph in the war with Egypt in 1967 but forced to resign after the losses Israel incurred in the October 1973 war with Syria. Her immigration and construction programs were the envy of the world, turning the "desert waste places into a garden."

A young Golda Meir, nd.
AP/Wide World Photos

A student of Walter Gropius while at Harvard, and a living icon of his profession, architect I.M. Pei continues to astound the world with his vision for structure. He has been associated with large-scale, multipurpose projects, urban revitalization, and cultural and educational buildings throughout his entire career. The East Building of the National Gallery of Art (1972) in Washington, D.C., the pyramids of the Louvre (1983) and the Concours Richelieu beneath them (1990), the John F. Kennedy Library (1979) and the Fragrant Hill Hotel in Beijing (1986) are dramatically arranged masses of glass, air, light, and soaring volumes of space.

The glass pyramids of the Louvre, Paris, France, designed by I.M. Pei. Photos courtesy offices of I.M. Pei; photo of the Louvre by Deide Von Schawen

Easter Monday (Can.) • MON *24*

IEOH MING PEI
Born in 1917 in
Canton, China

TUES *25*

Last Quarter Moon • I.M. Pei's Birthday • WED *26*

THURS *27*

April

S	M	T	W	T	F	S
						1
2	3	4	5	6	7	8
9	10	11	12	13	14	15
16	17	18	19	20	21	22
23	24	25	26	27	28	29
30						

FRI *28*

May

S	M	T	W	T	F	S
	1	2	3	4	5	6
7	8	9	10	11	12	13
14	15	16	17	18	19	20
21	22	23	24	25	26	27
28	29	30	31			

SAT *29*

SUN *30*

A&E

1 MON

2 TUES

SIGMUND FREUD
Born in 1856 in Pribor,
Czech Republic
(formerly Freiburg,
Moravia); d. 1939

3 WED • Golda Meir's Birthday, 1898

4 THURS • New Moon

May

S	M	T	W	T	F	S
	1	2	3	4	5	6
7	8	9	10	11	12	13
14	15	16	17	18	19	20
21	22	23	24	25	26	27
28	29	30	31			

5 FRI

6 SAT • Sigmund Freud's Birthday, 1856

June

S	M	T	W	T	F	S
				1	2	3
4	5	6	7	8	9	10
11	12	13	14	15	16	17
18	19	20	21	22	23	24
25	26	27	28	29	30	

7 SUN

Founder of psychoanalysis and contributor of diagnostic tools used to explore thoughts, dreams, and emotions, Sigmund Freud imposed a new understanding of humanity to an anxious public demanding explanations for mental and emotional illnesses. His emphasis on the sexual dynamic in human affairs—beginning in earliest childhood—put him at odds with the medical community for almost his whole life. In 1933 Hitler banned psychoanalysis, but permitted Freud and his family to emigrate to London, where he continued to write and treat his patients.

Martha Graham's visionary journey in dance so radically changed all areas of art that she has been classified with Pablo Picasso and Igor Stravinsky as one of the three seminal figures of 20th century arts. In 60 short years, she created a dramatic alternative to ballet, a classical technique that was much more than interpretive dance. Of her technique, Rudolf Nureyev said, "She made the vocabulary they all use." This vocabulary is part of a theater of costume, sets, and music that draw upon world art, yet remain intrinsically as American as Martha Graham's own roots (she was a direct descendant of Miles Standish). She changed the way women think of themselves, and the way in which the world thinks of women.

Martha Graham in 1938; photo © Barbara Morgan Photograph, Barbara Morgan Archives. Permission Martha Graham Center of Contemporary Dance

Harry S. Truman's Birthday, 1884 • MON **8**

MARTHA
GRAHAM
Born in 1894 in
Pittsburgh, Pa.;
d. 1991

TUES **9**

1st Quarter Moon • WED **10**

Martha Graham's Birthday, 1894 • THURS **11**

FRI **12**

May

S	M	T	W	T	F	S
	1	2	3	4	5	6
7	8	9	10	11	12	13
14	15	16	17	18	19	20
21	22	23	24	25	26	27
28	29	30	31			

SAT **13**

June

S	M	T	W	T	F	S
				1	2	3
4	5	6	7	8	9	10
11	12	13	14	15	16	17
18	19	20	21	22	23	24
25	26	27	28	29	30	

Mother's Day • SUN **14**

15 MON • Victoria Day (Can.)

16 TUES

17 WED

18 THURS • Full Moon • Pope John Paul II's Birthday, 1920

19 FRI

20 SAT • Armed Forces Day

21 SUN

JOHN PAUL II (born Karol Wojtyla)
Born in 1920 in Wadowice, Poland

May

S	M	T	W	T	F	S
	1	2	3	4	5	6
7	8	9	10	11	12	13
14	15	16	17	18	19	20
21	22	23	24	25	26	27
28	29	30	31			

June

S	M	T	W	T	F	S
				1	2	3
4	5	6	7	8	9	10
11	12	13	14	15	16	17
18	19	20	21	22	23	24
25	26	27	28	29	30	

A former poet and
actor in his extreme
youth, Pope John Paul
II is the first non-Italian
to be elected to the
papacy in over 450
years. Known as a
champion of justice and
an outspoken defender
of all religious rights,
he has traveled
extensively and boldly
challenged repressive
governments,
expressing his
authority on behalf of
the downtrodden. He is
viewed as something of
an *agent provocateur*
for the rights of man.

Pope John Paul II meditates
during the vigil at Aurora,
Colo., 1993.
AP/Wide World Photos

The haberdasher who became president, Harry Truman came to national attention by heading a committee that investigated government wartime production and thereby saved taxpayers millions of dollars. The prominence brought him to office as Franklin D. Roosevelt's vice president in 1945; he succeeded FDR in April of that year. The Truman Doctrine was a proposal for Communist containment and intended to support free peoples. He ordered the Berlin Airlift (1948), desegregated the armed forces (1948), established NATO (1949), and dismissed General Douglas MacArthur from his duties in the Far Eastern theater of war (1951). Known for his salty wit and the phrase, "The buck stops here."

Harry S. Truman and his bride, Bess Wallace Truman. Photos courtesy Harry S. Truman Library and AP/Wide World Photos

Victoria Day (Can.) • MON **22**

HARRY S. TRUMAN
Born in 1884 in
Lamar, Mo; d. 1972

TUES **23**

WED **24**

THURS **25**

May

S	M	T	W	T	F	S
	1	2	3	4	5	6
7	8	9	10	11	12	13
14	15	16	17	18	19	20
21	22	23	24	25	26	27
28	29	30	31			

Last Quarter Moon • FRI **26**

June

S	M	T	W	T	F	S
				1	2	3
4	5	6	7	8	9	10
11	12	13	14	15	16	17
18	19	20	21	22	23	24
25	26	27	28	29	30	

SAT **27**

SUN **28**

29 MON • Memorial Day (Observed) • Bob Hope's Birthday, 1903
• John F. Kennedy's Birthday, 1917

30 TUES

31 WED

1 THURS

2 FRI • New Moon

3 SAT

4 SUN

LESLIE TOWNES HOPE
Born in 1903 in London, England (emigrated to Cleveland at age four)

May

S	M	T	W	T	F	S
	1	2	3	4	5	6
7	8	9	10	11	12	13
14	15	16	17	18	19	20
21	22	23	24	25	26	27
28	29	30	31			

June

S	M	T	W	T	F	S
				1	2	3
4	5	6	7	8	9	10
11	12	13	14	15	16	17
18	19	20	21	22	23	24
25	26	27	28	29	30	

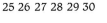

*P*utting his boundless optimism at the disposal of the armed forces, Bob Hope, America's greatest comedian, entertained the troops in peace and war and endeared himself in the hearts of people worldwide with his ski-jump nose, his lopsided grin, his railery at the absurdity of politics, and his natural, impeccable comedic timing. With costars Bing Crosby and Dorothy Lamour he made a series of *On the Road* films that are classics of their kind. In 1985 he was given the Kennedy Center Honors for Lifetime Achievement in the Arts.

Bob Hope on aging:

"Growing older means:
. . . feeling that if you were a car, you'd be recalled.
. . . going steady with your electric blanket.
. . . your favorite gourmet dish is prune souffle.
. . . the late show is the six o'clock news."

Bob Hope in Vietnam; photos courtesy Hope Enterprises, Inc.

$\mathscr{H}$orizontal lines, overhanging roofs, and a reverent use of regional materials characterize the designs of Frank Lloyd Wright, who today continues to embody the concept of architect as superstar. His was a total-concept vision in which he frequently took up the challenge to design and produce furnishings, textiles, fixtures, and accessories of living for his clients. He was among the first design practitioners to understand that an environment for living "develops from within outward." His most famous residence, Fallingwater, in Bear Run, Pa., has drawn thousands of devotees and tourists since it was completed in 1936; the spectacular Solomon R. Guggenheim Museum in New York City (completed in 1959) is perhaps his best-known public commission. He was a living symbol of flamboyant nerve, vision, and independence, celebrated American qualities that made him an international celebrity.

Fallingwater. Photo © Paul Rocheleau. OPPOSITE: The Frank Lloyd Wright Archives, Scottsdale, Ariz.

MON **5**

FRANK LLOYD
WRIGHT
Born in 1869 in
Richmond Center,
Wisc.; d. 1959

TUES **6**

WED **7**

1st Quarter Moon • Frank Lloyd Wright's Birthday, 1869 • THURS **8**

June

S	M	T	W	T	F	S
				1	2	3
4	5	6	7	8	9	10
11	12	13	14	15	16	17
18	19	20	21	22	23	24
25	26	27	28	29	30	

FRI **9**

July

S	M	T	W	T	F	S
						1
2	3	4	5	6	7	8
9	10	11	12	13	14	15
16	17	18	19	20	21	22
23	24	25	26	27	28	29
30	31					

SAT **10**

SUN **11**

12 MON

13 TUES

14 WED • Flag Day

15 THURS

16 FRI • Full Moon

17 SAT

18 SUN • Father's Day

JOHN FITZGERALD KENNEDY
Born in 1917 in Brookline, Mass.; d. 1963

June

S	M	T	W	T	F	S
				1	2	3
4	5	6	7	8	9	10
11	12	13	14	15	16	17
18	19	20	21	22	23	24
25	26	27	28	29	30	

July

S	M	T	W	T	F	S
						1
2	3	4	5	6	7	8
9	10	11	12	13	14	15
16	17	18	19	20	21	22
23	24	25	26	27	28	29
30	31					

Winner of the Pulitzer Prize for his 1956 book, *Profiles in Courage*, and the very popular 35th president, John F. Kennedy was descended from an Irish-American family that had demonstrated its talent for politics. His short term in office (only 1,000 days), was marked by altruism, patriotic fervor, and high drama. In 1962 the Cuban missile crisis led to the 1963 nuclear test ban treaty with the U.S.S.R. The Peace Corps inspired a generation of college-educated citizens to take up the problems of the Third World, fueling a missionary-style international outreach that continues today. He was assassinated in 1963.

Senator Kennedy in 1960 campaigning as presidential nominee. AP/Wide World Photos

Supreme Court Justice Thurgood Marshall, the great-grandson of a slave, graduated as valedictorian of Howard University Law School in 1933. Becoming a counsel for the NAACP in 1938, his work included establishing constitutional precedents in civil rights issues. Marshall argued the case of *Brown v. Board of Education* (1954), in which the Supreme Court overturned the then-accepted doctrine of separate but equal, thus ending segregation in public schools. President Kennedy named him to the U.S. Court of Appeals in 1962; President Johnson made him U.S. Solicitor General in 1965 and appointed him to the Supreme Court in 1967. He was succeeded by Clarence Thomas after resigning his position in 1991.

MON **19**

**THURGOOD
MARSHALL**
Born in 1908 in
Baltimore, Md.;
d. 1993

Summer begins • TUES **20**

WED **21**

THURS **22**

June

S	M	T	W	T	F	S
				1	2	3
4	5	6	7	8	9	10
11	12	13	14	15	16	17
18	19	20	21	22	23	24
25	26	27	28	29	30	

FRI **23**

July

S	M	T	W	T	F	S
						1
2	3	4	5	6	7	8
9	10	11	12	13	14	15
16	17	18	19	20	21	22
23	24	25	26	27	28	29
30	31					

Last Quarter Moon • SAT **24**

SUN **25**

26 MON

27 TUES

28 WED

29 THURS

30 FRI

1 SAT • Canada Day • New Moon • Estée Lauder's Birthday, 1908

2 SUN • Thurgood Marshall's Birthday, 1908

JOSEPHINE ESTHER MENTZER (Estée Lauder)
Born in 1908 in Corona, Queens, NY

June

S	M	T	W	T	F	S
				1	2	3
4	5	6	7	8	9	10
11	12	13	14	15	16	17
18	19	20	21	22	23	24
25	26	27	28	29	30	

July

S	M	T	W	T	F	S
						1
2	3	4	5	6	7	8
9	10	11	12	13	14	15
16	17	18	19	20	21	22
23	24	25	26	27	28	29
30	31					

A shrewd and razor-sharp marketing talent inspired Estée Lauder to offer free product samples to prospective customers. Her "Youth Dew" beauty oil which debuted in 1953, catapulted her into the multibillion cosmetics empire she and her son Leonard wield today. She defined an emerging sense of American "class" that had always relied on Europe for such distinctions. Her top-of-the-line packaging, top department store distribution channels, and pricing made her products sought-after emblems of prestige and success.

Photos courtesy the Lauder Family

Johnny Collins
PRESENTS
The International Star
Louis Armstrong

Gibson
CHICAGO

The cornet was the first instrument taken up by the trumpeter and jazz musician Louis Armstrong. He became identified with the Big Band sound in New Orleans, Chicago, and New York, where he also recorded with Bessie Smith. In 1930 his recording of the pop tune "Ain't Misbehavin'" became his first show business hit. Armstrong's All Stars, a Dixieland-style sextet, formed in 1947 and toured nationally and internationally until his death in 1971, bringing a unique American sound to a world that adored his rich, humorous take on music.

Louis Armstrong 1941. Photos Louis Armstrong House and Archives Queens College/CUNY. Permission Louis Armstrong Educational Foundation

MON 3

LOUIS "SATCHMO" ARMSTRONG
Born ca. 1901 in New Orleans, La.; d. 1971

Independence Day • Louis Armstrong's Birthday, ca. 1901 • TUES 4

WED 5

THURS 6

July

S	M	T	W	T	F	S
						1
2	3	4	5	6	7	8
9	10	11	12	13	14	15
16	17	18	19	20	21	22
23	24	25	26	27	28	29
30	31					

FRI 7

August

S	M	T	W	T	F	S
		1	2	3	4	5
6	7	8	9	10	11	12
13	14	15	16	17	18	19
20	21	22	23	24	25	26
27	28	29	30	31		

1st Quarter Moon • SAT 8

SUN 9

10 MON

11 TUES

12 WED

13 THURS

14 FRI

15 SAT

16 SUN • Full Moon

ERNEST MILLER HEMINGWAY
Born in 1899 in Oak Park, Ill.; d. 1961

July

S	M	T	W	T	F	S
						1
2	3	4	5	6	7	8
9	10	11	12	13	14	15
16	17	18	19	20	21	22
23	24	25	26	27	28	29
30	31					

August

S	M	T	W	T	F	S
		1	2	3	4	5
6	7	8	9	10	11	12
13	14	15	16	17	18	19
20	21	22	23	24	25	26
27	28	29	30	31		

The Pulitzer Prize was awarded to Ernest Hemingway in 1952 for his novella, *The Old Man and the Sea*, and in 1954 he was awarded the Nobel Prize for Literature. The recognition came near the end of his career as the great revitalizer of American literary style. A spokesman for the so-called Lost Generation, Hemingway developed a reputation for fast living that was captured in the press worldwide. His training as a journalist prepared him for work as a correspondent during the Spanish civil war. His terse prose, macho-style self-promotion, and astute networking of the social power sources after World War II prefigured the modern obsession with the media that writers still grapple with today.

Ernest Hemingway wounded at age nineteen while driving an ambulance in World War I. Under exclusive license with Hemingway, Ltd., through Fashion Licensing of America, Inc., NY. AP/Wide World Photos

Amelia Earhart
Given by her
Mother
1940

Aviator Amelia Earhart worked as a nurse's aide in Toronto, attended several schools, including two stints at Columbia University, and held odd jobs in California. By 1921, Earhart made her first solo flight. By 1928 she participated in a transatlantic flight with Wilmer Stultz and Louis Gordon, becoming the first woman to cross the Atlantic in an airplane. In 1932 she flew the transatlantic route alone, in a record-setting time of 14 hours, 56 minutes. By 1937 she had become a national favorite. Her project to circumnavigate the globe turned that year to tragedy after she left New Guinea with her navigator Frederick Noonan on July 2. The mystery of their disappearance haunts aviation experts and historians even today, as new details continue to emerge from expeditions determined to locate her plane.

MON **17**

AMELIA MARY
EARHART
Born 1898 in
Atchison, Kans.;
d. 1937

TUES **18**

WED **19**

THURS **20**

July

S	M	T	W	T	F	S
						1
2	3	4	5	6	7	8
9	10	11	12	13	14	15
16	17	18	19	20	21	22
23	24	25	26	27	28	29
30	31					

Ernest Hemingway's Birthday, 1899 • FRI **21**

August

S	M	T	W	T	F	S
		1	2	3	4	5
6	7	8	9	10	11	12
13	14	15	16	17	18	19
20	21	22	23	24	25	26
27	28	29	30	31		

SAT **22**

SUN **23**

24 MON • Last Quarter Moon • Amelia Earhart's Birthday, 1898

25 TUES

JACQUELINE LEE BOUVIER KENNEDY ONASSIS

Born in 1929 in Southampton, NY; d. 1994

26 WED

27 THURS

28 FRI • Jacqueline Kennedy Onassis' Birthday, 1929

July

S	M	T	W	T	F	S
						1
2	3	4	5	6	7	8
9	10	11	12	13	14	15
16	17	18	19	20	21	22
23	24	25	26	27	28	29
30	31					

29 SAT

August

S	M	T	W	T	F	S
		1	2	3	4	5
6	7	8	9	10	11	12
13	14	15	16	17	18	19
20	21	22	23	24	25	26
27	28	29	30	31		

30 SUN • New Moon • Henry Ford's Birthday, 1863

A strong, personal flair expressed through elegance and a discriminating attention to detail was just one of the strengths Jacqueline Bouvier Kennedy Onassis brought to every dimension of her life. Finding herself in the thrilling position as First Lady in 1961, she brought to bear her educated, international, "high-society" background to refurbish a dowdy White House with a curator's sureness, knowledge, and skill. Her natural qualities of intelligence combined with her intense social abilities won the hearts of even her critics, who wanted to dismiss her tenacious vision of American style. Her unflinching courage and undeviating control of tradition that surrounded the President's funeral revealed her true-grit realism to the world and won her great admiration. Her marriage to shipping magnate Aristotle Onassis stunned America. After his death she pursued a restrained, dignified professional life as an editor with a major book publisher. Hers is a legacy of individualism and grace under extreme pressure.

Jacqueline Lee Bouvier marries Senator John F. Kennedy, 1953. AP/Wide World Photos

everyone will be famous for 15 minutes" was the prediction of artist Andy Warhol, acknowledged as a founder of the heady and irreverent Pop Art movement of the 1960s. He sought to reposition great visual icons of America's pervasive graphic arts, utilizing comic strips and bubble gum colorings, commercial product labels such as soup cans and newsprint. From painting he moved to film, evoking the same level of shock value from the banal to the outrageous. He assembled an impressive collection of antique furniture and was an obsessive collector. His legacy of color-saturated multiples of celebrities became a signature style.

Andy Warhol. Self Portrait, 1967. Synthetic polymer paint and silkscreen ink on canvas. 72x72 in. © 1999 The Andy Warhol Foundation for the Visual Arts, Inc. Courtesy

MON *31*

ANDY WARHOL
Born in 1928 in
Pittsburgh, Pa.;
d. 1987

TUES *1*

WED *2*

THURS *3*

July

S	M	T	W	T	F	S
						1
2	3	4	5	6	7	8
9	10	11	12	13	14	15
16	17	18	19	20	21	22
23	24	25	26	27	28	29
30	31					

FRI *4*

SAT *5*

August

S	M	T	W	T	F	S
		1	2	3	4	5
6	7	8	9	10	11	12
13	14	15	16	17	18	19
20	21	22	23	24	25	26
27	28	29	30	31		

1st Quarter Moon • Andy Warhol's Birthday, 1928 • **SUN** *6*

A&E

7   MON • Civic Holiday (Can.)

8   TUES

9   WED

10   THURS

11   FRI

12   SAT

13   SUN • Alfred Hitchcock's Birthday, 1899

HENRY FORD
Born in 1863 in
Dearborn, Mich.;
d. 1947

August

S	M	T	W	T	F	S
		1	2	3	4	5
6	7	8	9	10	11	12
13	14	15	16	17	18	19
20	21	22	23	24	25	26
27	28	29	30	31		

September

S	M	T	W	T	F	S
					1	2
3	4	5	6	7	8	9
10	11	12	13	14	15	16
17	18	19	20	21	22	23
24	25	26	27	28	29	30

$\mathcal{B}$y 1928 Henry Ford had sold 15 million Model T automobiles, thereby putting America on wheels. The American industrialist created three manufacturing techniques which brought unparalleled prosperity to working-class citizens: he adapted the conveyor belt to bring materials to the worker, he devised completely interchangeable parts, and he streamlined the assembly line production process so that almost any individual could step in and run it. He also publicized his new techniques, thus raising the entire level of American industrial production methods, increasing the income level of countless laborers.

Photos courtesy Henry Ford Museum, Dearborn, Mich.

"To boldly go where no man has gone before . . ." the famous challenge from the captain of the crew of the Starship *Enterprise*, is the legacy to our planet from Gene Roddenberry, the creator and producer of *Star Trek*, the 1960s television series whose six subsequent film spin-offs the world still enjoys today. Roddenberry's careers included being a bomber pilot, a TWA airline pilot, a police officer, and writing scripts for television's *Dragnet* in his spare time. Though he is credited for creating the line, "Beam me up, Scotty," knowledgeable Trekkies say the words were never spoken by Captain Kirk, Spock, Bones, or anybody else on the show—illustrating the fanatic dedication to *Star Trek* detail by his fans.

Photos courtesy Majel Barrett Roddenberry

MON **14**

**EUGENE WESLEY
RODDENBERRY**
Born 1921 in El Paso,
Tex.; d. 1991

Full Moon • TUES **15**

WED **16**

THURS **17**

August

S	M	T	W	T	F	S
		1	2	3	4	5
6	7	8	9	10	11	12
13	14	15	16	17	18	19
20	21	22	23	24	25	26
27	28	29	30	31		

FRI **18**

September

S	M	T	W	T	F	S
					1	2
3	4	5	6	7	8	9
10	11	12	13	14	15	16
17	18	19	20	21	22	23
24	25	26	27	28	29	30

Orville Wright's Birthday, 1871 • Coco Chanel's Birthday, 1882 • SAT **19**
Gene Roddenberry's Birthday, 1921

SUN **20**

A&E

21 MON

22 TUES • Last Quarter Moon

23 WED

24 THURS

25 FRI

26 SAT • Peggy Guggenheim's Birthday, 1898

27 SUN • Mother Teresa's Birthday, 1910

PEGGY (born Marguerite) GUGGENHEIM
Born 1898 in New York City; d. 1979

August

S	M	T	W	T	F	S
		1	2	3	4	5
6	7	8	9	10	11	12
13	14	15	16	17	18	19
20	21	22	23	24	25	26
27	28	29	30	31		

September

S	M	T	W	T	F	S
					1	2
3	4	5	6	7	8	9
10	11	12	13	14	15	16
17	18	19	20	21	22	23
24	25	26	27	28	29	30

Peggy Guggenheim was a major American figure in fostering artistic ties between Europe and the United States in the 20th century. Born in New York City, Guggenheim was a Parisian bohemian in her youth and later a gallery owner in London and New York—where she established her avant-garde gallery, Art of This Century. The last thirty years of her life were spent in her home in Palazzo Venier dei Leoni in Venice, where she realized her ambition to open a museum of modern art that included major artistic movements of the 20th century such as Cubism, European abstraction, Surrealism, and early American Abstract Expressionism. She donated her Palazzo and collection to the Solomon R. Guggenheim Foundation in New York, which permanently exhibits her collection in Venice as a testimonial of its excellence. Guggenheim was a collector and a patron of some of the most innovative and provocative artists of the early 20th century. Among the artists whose works are in her museum are Constantin Brancusi, Salvador Dali, Max Ernst, Alberto Giacometti, Arshile Gorky, Vasily Kandinsky, Joan Miro, Robert Motherwell, Pablo Picasso, and Jackson Pollock.

Photo by Roloff Beny, National Archives, Canada.
OPPOSITE: photo Peggy Guggenheim late 1930s
© The Solomon R. Guggenheim Foundation, NY

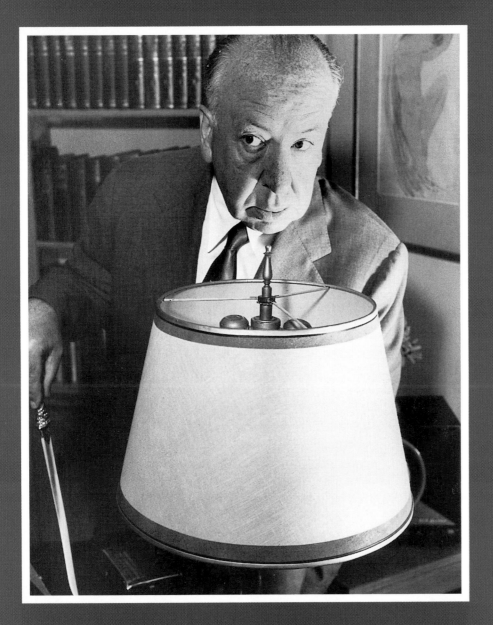

*P*erceiving that movies were capable of far more subtlety and persuasiveness than was being delivered at the time, film director Alfred Hitchcock raised the heat considerably by bringing unconscious fears and aggressions onto the big screen. An enigma himself, he became the honored innovator and subsequent master of the psychological thriller, *Psycho* (1960) being the masterpiece of his oeuvre. *Frenzy* (1972) and *The Birds* (1963) gave the public nightmares, and for these and other masterworks of suspense he was knighted in 1980.

SIR ALFRED JOSEPH HITCHCOCK
Born in 1899 in London, England; d. 1980

MON **28**

New Moon • TUES **29**

WED **30**

THURS **31**

FRI **1**

SAT **2**

SUN **3**

August

S	M	T	W	T	F	S
		1	2	3	4	5
6	7	8	9	10	11	12
13	14	15	16	17	18	19
20	21	22	23	24	25	26
27	28	29	30	31		

September

S	M	T	W	T	F	S
					1	2
3	4	5	6	7	8	9
10	11	12	13	14	15	16
17	18	19	20	21	22	23
24	25	26	27	28	29	30

4 MON • Labor Day • Labour Day (Can.)

5 TUES • 1st Quarter Moon

GABRIELLE CHANEL
Born in 1883 in Saumur, France, an orphan; d. 1971

6 WED

7 THURS

8 FRI

September

S	M	T	W	T	F	S
					1	2
3	4	5	6	7	8	9
10	11	12	13	14	15	16
17	18	19	20	21	22	23
24	25	26	27	28	29	30

9 SAT

October

S	M	T	W	T	F	S
1	2	3	4	5	6	7
8	9	10	11	12	13	14
15	16	17	18	19	20	21
22	23	24	25	26	27	28
29	30	31				

10 SUN

The collarless cardigan jacket and the notion of trousers for women launched Coco Chanel into the stratosphere of international fashion. Noted for simple jersey dresses and suits, two perfumes, black or gray pullovers with white pique collars and cuffs, frankly fake costume jewelry mixed in with the real stuff, camellias, and her endless French cigarettes, Chanel redefined comfortable clothes for the rich, athletic, uninhibited, post-World-War-I woman.

Coco Chanel and Chanel No. 5 Parfum. Photos courtesy Chanel, Inc.

N°5
CHANEL
PARFUM

*M*other Teresa began caring for those in need in 1928 with a slum school to teach the children of the poor. But when she and her former pupils found men, women, and children dying on the streets of Calcutta, they took them to hospitals, sometimes in a wheelbarrow, and when the hospitals were full, they rented a room where they could care for them. In 1950 the Missionaries of Charity was established by the Catholic Church, and Mother Teresa and the sisters took, in addition to the three vows of poverty, chastity, and obedience, a fourth vow: to give wholehearted and free service to the poorest of the poor. She received medical training in Paris that equipped her to help lepers and to be of assistance in the aftermath of natural disasters. She was awarded the Pope John XXIII Peace Prize in 1971 and the Nobel Peace Prize in 1979.

Mother Teresa 1989; The Missionaries of Charity kindly grant permission for use of this photo; photo by Michael Collopy, © 1998

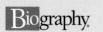 

MON **11**

**MOTHER TERESA
OF CALCUTTA**
Born in 1910 in
Skopje, Yugoslavia;
d. 1997

TUES **12**

Full Moon • WED **13**

THURS **14**

September

S	M	T	W	T	F	S
					1	2
3	4	5	6	7	8	9
10	11	12	13	14	15	16
17	18	19	20	21	22	23
24	25	26	27	28	29	30

FRI **15**

October

S	M	T	W	T	F	S
1	2	3	4	5	6	7
8	9	10	11	12	13	14
15	16	17	18	19	20	21
22	23	24	25	26	27	28
29	30	31				

SAT **16**

SUN **17**

18 MON • Agnes deMille's Birthday, 1905

AGNES GEORGE DEMILLE
Born in 1905 in New York City; d. 1993

19 TUES

20 WED • Last Quarter Moon

21 THURS

22 FRI • Autumn Begins

September

S	M	T	W	T	F	S
					1	2
3	4	5	6	7	8	9
10	11	12	13	14	15	16
17	18	19	20	21	22	23
24	25	26	27	28	29	30

23 SAT

October

S	M	T	W	T	F	S
1	2	3	4	5	6	7
8	9	10	11	12	13	14
15	16	17	18	19	20	21
22	23	24	25	26	27	28
29	30	31				

24 SUN

A&E

The choreographer of one of America's favorite musicals *Oklahoma* (1943), Agnes deMille began her career as an actress and a dancer. She received her first commission in 1936 when she was asked to design a dance sequence for the British film *Romeo and Juliet*. Her stage work also includes *Rodeo* (1942), *Carousel* (1945), *Brigadoon* (1947), and *Gentlemen Prefer Blondes* (1949). Her training in classical ballet brought a new expression of elegance to the Broadway stage at a time when vaudeville still reigned. DeMille changed the experience of musicals in a way similar to the reinterpretations of choreographers like Bob Fosse and Jerome Robbins. In her "spare time" she wrote *Dance to the Piper* (1951) and *And Promenade Home* (1956), as well as a biography of Martha Graham (1991).

Agnes deMille in Rodeo. *Photos Culver Pictures, Inc.*

*L*yricist Ira Gershwin was older brother to composer George, with whom he began his long collaboration in 191? George Gershwin played both popular and classical piano in childhood. His first big hit, "Swanee," appeared in 1919. The brothers won a Pulitzer Prize for the musical *Of Thee Sing* in 1931. George Gershwin cherished a hope that commercial and classical genres of music could be united, resulting in his histor: jazz-oriented classic works *Rhapsody in Blue* (1924), *An American in Paris* (1928), an *Porgy and Bess* (1935). Though Tin Pan Alley was th school in which George Gershwin's genius was readi understood, modern musicologists agree that Ira's lyrics added a distinctive very and style to the uniquely American musical form.

George and Ira Gershwin in 1936 arriving at the Los Angeles airport. Photo courtesy of Ira and Leonore Gershwin Trusts. Used by permission

MON 25

ISRAEL
GERSHWIN
Born 1896 in
Brooklyn, NY; d. 1983

GEORGE
GERSHWIN
Born 1898 in
Brooklyn, NY; d. 1937

George Gershwin's Birthday, 1898 • TUES 26

New Moon • WED 27

THURS 28

September

S	M	T	W	T	F	S
					1	2
3	4	5	6	7	8	9
10	11	12	13	14	15	16
17	18	19	20	21	22	23
24	25	26	27	28	29	30

FRI 29

October

S	M	T	W	T	F	S
1	2	3	4	5	6	7
8	9	10	11	12	13	14
15	16	17	18	19	20	21
22	23	24	25	26	27	28
29	30	31				

Rosh Hashanah • SAT 30

SUN 1

2 MON • Groucho Marx's Birthday, 1895 • Mohandas Gandhi's Birthday, 1869

3 TUES

4 WED

5 THURS • 1st Quarter Moon • Robert Goddard's Birthday, 1882

6 FRI

7 SAT

8 SUN

JULIUS HENRY "GROUCHO" MARX
Born in 1895 in New York City; d. 1977

October

S	M	T	W	T	F	S
1	2	3	4	5	6	7
8	9	10	11	12	13	14
15	16	17	18	19	20	21
22	23	24	25	26	27	28
29	30	31				

November

S	M	T	W	T	F	S
				1	2	3	4
5	6	7	8	9	10	11
12	13	14	15	16	17	18
19	20	21	22	23	24	25
26	27	28	29	30		

Of the five Marx Brothers, Groucho rose to the greatest national prominence, ending his career with his own television show and the phrase, "Say the 'Secret Word' and win $100." *You Bet Your Life* was a weekly ritual for millions of Americans who adored Groucho's earthy, low-brow humor in the early days of national television. His brothers Chico, Harpo, Gummo, and Zeppo appeared with him in the early days of filmmaking. Critics and admirers from T.S. Eliot to Johnny Carson lauded the Marx Brothers as zany, madcap artists who originated a uniquely American brand of entertainment.

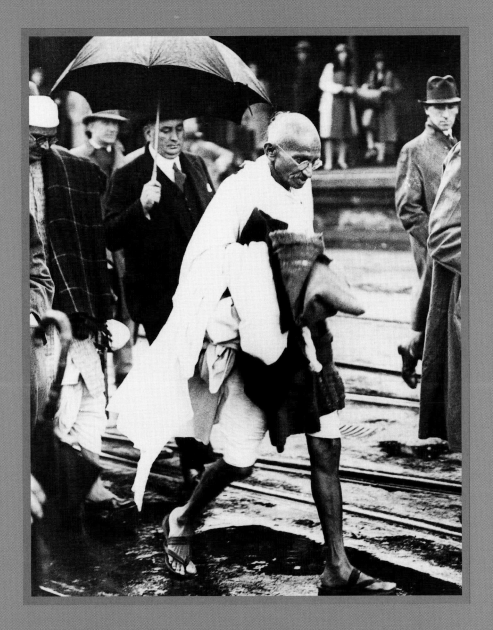

A master of strategies using methods of nonviolent civil disobedience, Mohandas Gandhi was the Indian nationalist leader who goaded and guided his country's citizens toward independence of British rule. He studied law in London, practiced it in South Africa, and entered politics in India by strongly supporting home rule. After "Freedom at Midnight," in 1947, he tried to stop the horrific Hindu-Muslim conflict that ultimately led to the partitioning of India and the creation of Pakistan. An assassin shot him while at prayer in 1948.

AP/Wide World Photos

Columbus Day (Observed) • Yom Kippur • Thanksgiving Day (Can.) • MON **9**

MOHANDAS
KARAMCHAND
GANDHI
Born in 1869 in
Poorbandar,
Kathiawar, India;
d. 1948

TUES **10**

Eleanor Roosevelt's Birthday, 1884 • WED **11**

Columbus Day • THURS **12**

*O*ctober

S	M	T	W	T	F	S
1	2	3	4	5	6	7
8	9	10	11	12	13	14
15	16	17	18	19	20	21
22	23	24	25	26	27	28
29	30	31				

Full Moon • Margaret Thatcher's Birthday, 1925 • FRI **13**

*N*ovember

S	M	T	W	T	F	S
			1	2	3	4
5	6	7	8	9	10	11
12	13	14	15	16	17	18
19	20	21	22	23	24	25
26	27	28	29	30		

Dwight Eisenhower's Birthday, 1879 • SAT **14**

SUN **15**

October

16 MON

17 TUES

18 WED

19 THURS

20 FRI • Last Quarter Moon

21 SAT

22 SUN • Daylight Savings Time ends

ROBERT HUTCHINGS GODDARD
Born in 1882 in Worcester, Mass.; d. 1945

October

S	M	T	W	T	F	S
1	2	3	4	5	6	7
8	9	10	11	12	13	14
15	16	17	18	19	20	21
22	23	24	25	26	27	28
29	30	31				

November

S	M	T	W	T	F	S
			1	2	3	4
5	6	7	8	9	10	11
12	13	14	15	16	17	18
19	20	21	22	23	24	25
26	27	28	29	30		

Funded by no less than the Smithsonian Institution during the period of his early work on solid-fuel rocketry, and encouraged by no less a national hero than Charles Lindbergh, Robert Goddard was a space pioneer. He launched the world's first liquid-fuel rocket in 1926, which eventually led to a testing laboratory developed for him in Roswell, N.M. His legacy to world rocket technology includes 200 patents, much of which predates discoveries made by German rocket scientists before World War II. His papers are kept at the Goddard Library at Clark University in Worcester, Mass.

Goddard and liquid oxygen-gasoline rocket in frame from which it was first fired on March 16, 1926. Photos courtesy Clark University, Goddard Library

*J*onas Salk's pathbreaking studies on viruses and principles of immunization led to the first effective vaccine against the dreaded paralytic poliomyelitis. (In 1952 alone, the polio virus struck more than 50,000 people in America.) Approved for general use in 1955, the noninfectious, injected killed-poliovirus vaccine developed by Salk and his colleagues at the University of Pittsburgh reduced the U.S. incidence of polio 95% by 1961. This vaccine and Albert Sabin's infectious, oral live poliovirus vaccine, first widely used in the U.S. in 1962, promise to eradicate crippling polio from the world within the next decade. Today, the Salk Institute for biological Studies in La Jolla, Calif., founded by Salk in 1963, is one of the world's leading biological research centers. Salk received a special congressional medal (1956), the Lasker Award (1956), and the nation's highest civilian honor, The Presidential Medal of Freedom (1977).

Dr. Salk and his family in 1955 at the Pittsburgh airport just after the announcement the polio vaccine was safe and effective. Photos courtesy the Jonas Salk Trust

MON _23_

JONAS SALK, M.D.
Born in 1914 in New
York City; d. 1995

TUES _24_

Pablo Picasso's Birthday, 1881 • WED _25_

THURS _26_

October

S	M	T	W	T	F	S
1	2	3	4	5	6	7
8	9	10	11	12	13	14
15	16	17	18	19	20	21
22	23	24	25	26	27	28
29	30	31				

New Moon • Bill Gates' Birthday, 1955 • FRI _27_

Jonas Salk's Birthday, 1914 • SAT _28_

November

S	M	T	W	T	F	S
				1	2	3	4
5	6	7	8	9	10	11
12	13	14	15	16	17	18
19	20	21	22	23	24	25
26	27	28	29	30		

SUN _29_

Biography.

30 MON

31 TUES • Halloween

WILLIAM H. GATES
Born in 1955 in Seattle, Wash.

1 WED

2 THURS

3 FRI

October

S	M	T	W	T	F	S
1	2	3	4	5	6	7
8	9	10	11	12	13	14
15	16	17	18	19	20	21
22	23	24	25	26	27	28
29	30	31				

4 SAT • 1st Quarter Moon

November

S	M	T	W	T	F	S
			1	2	3	4
5	6	7	8	9	10	11
12	13	14	15	16	17	18
19	20	21	22	23	24	25
26	27	28	29	30		

5 SUN

A&E.

A pioneering architect of the Information Age, Bill Gates dropped out of Harvard to cofound Microsoft in 1975. His vision: to make software that would put a computer on every desk and in every home. Microsoft's MS-DOS operating system for PCs and its successor, Windows, subsequently became the most popular in the world, and Microsoft swiftly grew into America's leading software company. As the Internet has transformed the computer industry, Gates has reinvented Microsoft around it, confirming him as one of the leading technological and business strategists of our time.

Bill Gates 1998 photo by Michael O'Neill. Photos courtesy Microsoft

Humanitarian Eleanor Roosevelt was a distant cousin of her husband Franklin (president of the United States, 1933–1945). With his election she emerged as a truly public figure in her own right, traveling, lecturing, and broadcasting on behalf of the downtrodden of the world, of which there were many during the aftermath of the Great Depression. She worked for the Red Cross, served as a delegate to the U.N. General Assembly, and was chairperson of the U.N.'s Human Rights Commission. In 1961 she chaired President John F. Kennedy's Commission on the Status of Women. Her syndicated newspaper column, "My Day" began in 1935.

Photos courtesy the Franklin D. Roosevelt Library

MON **6**

ANNA ELEANOR ROOSEVELT
Born in 1884 in New York City; d. 1962

Election Day • TUES **7**

WED **8**

THURS **9**

November

S	M	T	W	T	F	S
			1	2	3	4
5	6	7	8	9	10	11
12	13	14	15	16	17	18
19	20	21	22	23	24	25
26	27	28	29	30		

FRI **10**

December

S	M	T	W	T	F	S
					1	2
3	4	5	6	7	8	9
10	11	12	13	14	15	16
17	18	19	20	21	22	23
24	25	26	27	28	29	30
31						

Veterans Day • Remembrance Day (Can.) • Full Moon • SAT **11**

SUN **12**

13 MON

14 TUES

MARGARET HILDA
THATCHER, Baroness
Thatcher of Kesteven
(born Roberts).
Born in 1925 in Grantham,
Lincolnshire, England

15 WED

16 THURS

17 FRI

18 SAT • Last Quarter Moon

19 SUN

Replacing Edward Heath in 1975 as leader of the Conservative
Party, Margaret Thatcher became the first woman party leader in
British politics. Upon becoming prime minister in 1979, Thatcher
brought about policy changes that polarized society but rescued the
nation from industrial paralysis and potential financial collapse. She
remained in office through two more elections, and by 1988 was the
longest-serving prime minister in English history. She was unseated
in 1990 because of her views regarding England's partnership with a
united European currency and strife within her party. She was called
the "Iron Maiden" by friends and foes alike. Revered and reviled,
Lady Thatcher deftly guided Britain through chaotic times.

AP/Wide World Photos

As a player on the world stage, America's 34th president, Dwight D. Eisenhower, adopted a low-profile approach which won him respect and admiration as the challenges of his presidency emerged: the Korean War stalemate in 1953, the policy to contain communist expansion, and the convulsive early stages of the civil rights movement. He was not the first military general to win the presidency, but he was the first to warn of the danger of what came to be known as the military-industrial complex. Despite his warnings, future presidents would endorse America's participation in the war in Indochina.

INSET: Dwight D. Eisenhower with his bride, Mamie Geneva Doud, after their wedding, 1916. General Eisenhower, Kansas City, 1945. AP/Wide World Photos

MON 20

DWIGHT DAVID
EISENHOWER
Born in 1890 in
Denison, Tex.; d. 1969

TUES 21

WED 22

Thanksgiving • THURS 23

November

S	M	T	W	T	F	S
			1	2	3	4
5	6	7	8	9	10	11
12	13	14	15	16	17	18
19	20	21	22	23	24	25
26	27	28	29	30		

FRI 24

December

S	M	T	W	T	F	S
					1	2
3	4	5	6	7	8	9
10	11	12	13	14	15	16
17	18	19	20	21	22	23
24	25	26	27	28	29	30
31						

New Moon • SAT 25

SUN 26

27 MON • Jimi Hendrix's Birthday, 1942

28 TUES

JAMES MARSHALL HENDRIX
Born 1942 in Seattle, Wash.; d. 1970

29 WED

30 THURS • Winston Churchill's Birthday, 1874

November

S	M	T	W	T	F	S
			1	2	3	4
5	6	7	8	9	10	11
12	13	14	15	16	17	18
19	20	21	22	23	24	25
26	27	28	29	30		

1 FRI

December

S	M	T	W	T	F	S
					1	2
3	4	5	6	7	8	9
10	11	12	13	14	15	16
17	18	19	20	21	22	23
24	25	26	27	28	29	30
31						

2 SAT

3 SUN • 1st Quarter Moon

$\mathcal{H}$ailed as the greatest guitarist of all time, Jimi Hendrix remains one of the most important musicians in the history of popular music. Signature songs such as "Purple Haze" and "Voodoo Child (Slight Return)" continue to inspire musicians of every genre throughout the world. His untimely death in September 1970, robbed popular music of one of its brightest innovators.

Esteemed by some of the finest art critics as the seminal influence of the 20th century in painting, Pablo Picasso remains the dominant figure of modern art. As a young man he came from Spain to set up his first studio in Paris at a period of converging influences, which he both affected and was affected by. Throughout his career he reinvented himself countless times, exploring every medium that came into his hands—sculpture, ceramics, photography, lithography, costume and stage set design. A recent emphasis on his portraitur has brought his vast assemblage to public attention once again.

Picasso, Pablo, Woman with Raised Arms, 1936. © ARS, NY, Private Collection. Permission Artist Rights Society, NY. Photo Culver Pictures, Inc.

December

MON **4**

PABLO PICASSO
Born in 1881 in
Malaga, Spain; d. 1973

Walt Disney's Birthday, 1901 • TUES **5**

WED **6**

THURS **7**

December

S	M	T	W	T	F	S
					1	2
3	4	5	6	7	8	9
10	11	12	13	14	15	16
17	18	19	20	21	22	23
24	25	26	27	28	29	30
31						

FRI **8**

SAT **9**

January 2001

S	M	T	W	T	F	S
	1	2	3	4	5	6
7	8	9	10	11	12	13
14	15	16	17	18	19	20
21	22	23	24	25	26	27
28	29	30	31			

SUN **10**

11 MON • Full Moon

12 TUES

MARGARET MEAD
Born in 1901 in Philadelphia, Pa.; d. 1978

13 WED

14 THURS

15 FRI

December

S	M	T	W	T	F	S
					1	2
3	4	5	6	7	8	9
10	11	12	13	14	15	16
17	18	19	20	21	22	23
24	25	26	27	28	29	30
31						

16 SAT • Margaret Mead's Birthday, 1901

January 2001

S	M	T	W	T	F	S
	1	2	3	4	5	6
7	8	9	10	11	12	13
14	15	16	17	18	19	20
21	22	23	24	25	26	27
28	29	30	31			

17 SUN • Last Quarter Moon

*R*elinquishing nothing of her strong academic background and training, cultural anthropologist Margaret Mead was able to cross over to mainstream populist reading with her brilliant book *Coming of Age in Samoa* (1928), a landmark study of sexual mores in a primitive society the world knew little about. Her work had an impact on broadening popular concepts of appropriate sexual behavior and development at a time when Sigmund Freud's research was considered sensational. Among the first professional women activists, Dr. Mead brought an awareness to well-educated women of their obligation to help improve the national climate for economic advancement and career opportunities for all working people.

Dr. Margaret Mead in the Admiralty Islands, 1954, courtesy the Institute for Intercultural Studies, NY. AP/Wide World Photos

"*Never*, never, never give up!" may be the most famous saying of British statesman, orator, two-time prime minister, journalist, painter, and author of histories, Winston Churchill. Described in his later years as "the greatest living Englishman," Churchill came to symbolize a national resilience strengthened with tenacity that gave heart to a Britain struggling with the privations and horrors of World War II. He won the Nobel Prize for Literature in the same year he was knighted, 1953.

Winston Churchill at a favorite hobby, 1949.
AP/Wide World Photos

MON **18**

SIR WINSTON
LEONARD
SPENCER
CHURCHILL
Born in 1874 at
Blenheim Palace,
Oxfordshire, England;
d. 1965

TUES **19**

WED **20**

Winter begins • THURS **21**

December

S	M	T	W	T	F	S
					1	2
3	4	5	6	7	8	9
10	11	12	13	14	15	16
17	18	19	20	21	22	23
24	25	26	27	28	29	30
31						

Hanukkah • FRI **22**

SAT **23**

January 2001

S	M	T	W	T	F	S
	1	2	3	4	5	6
7	8	9	10	11	12	13
14	15	16	17	18	19	20
21	22	23	24	25	26	27
28	29	30	31			

SUN **24**

25 MON • Christmas • New Moon

26 TUES • Boxing Day (Can.)

WOODROW THOMAS WILSON
Born in 1856 in Staunton, Va.; d. 1924

27 WED

28 THURS • Woodrow Wilson's Birthday, 1856

29 FRI

December

S	M	T	W	T	F	S
					1	2
3	4	5	6	7	8	9
10	11	12	13	14	15	16
17	18	19	20	21	22	23
24	25	26	27	28	29	30
31						

30 SAT

January 2001

S	M	T	W	T	F	S
	1	2	3	4	5	6
7	8	9	10	11	12	13
14	15	16	17	18	19	20
21	22	23	24	25	26	27
28	29	30	31			

31 SUN

His first presidency was that of Princeton University in 1902. Even then his sense of reform was active, drawing him into politics to the extent that he was elected governor of New Jersey by 1911. Woodrow Wilson, the 28th president of the United States, benefited from a rift between William Howard Taft and Theodore Roosevelt, allowing the Democratic candidate a landslide victory in 1912. His initiatives that we live with today include the graduated income tax, the eight-hour workday, and his landmark laws controlling child labor. After World War I, Wilson devoted tremendous energy to world peace. He supported the League of Nations, but failed to convince an increasingly isolationist America. His visionary treaty was ultimately defeated in Congress. Wilson retired to seclusion in 1921, one of this country's most intelligent and intransigent public officials.

Photo courtesy the Woodrow Wilson Museum, Staunton, Va.

1999

JANUARY
```
M  T  W  T  F  S  S
            1  2  3
 4  5  6  7  8  9 10
11 12 13 14 15 16 17
18 19 20 21 22 23 24
25 26 27 28 29 30 31
```

FEBRUARY
```
M  T  W  T  F  S  S
 1  2  3  4  5  6  7
 8  9 10 11 12 13 14
15 16 17 18 19 20 21
22 23 24 25 26 27 28
```

MARCH
```
M  T  W  T  F  S  S
 1  2  3  4  5  6  7
 8  9 10 11 12 13 14
15 16 17 18 19 20 21
22 23 24 25 26 27 28
29 30 31
```

APRIL
```
M  T  W  T  F  S  S
             1  2  3  4
 5  6  7  8  9 10 11
12 13 14 15 16 17 18
19 20 21 22 23 24 25
26 27 28 29 30
```

MAY
```
M  T  W  T  F  S  S
                1  2
 3  4  5  6  7  8  9
10 11 12 13 14 15 16
17 18 19 20 21 22 23
24 25 26 27 28 29 30
31
```

JUNE
```
M  T  W  T  F  S  S
    1  2  3  4  5  6
 7  8  9 10 11 12 13
14 15 16 17 18 19 20
21 22 23 24 25 26 27
28 29 30
```

JULY
```
M  T  W  T  F  S  S
          1  2  3  4
 5  6  7  8  9 10 11
12 13 14 15 16 17 18
19 20 21 22 23 24 25
26 27 28 29 30 31
```

AUGUST
```
M  T  W  T  F  S  S
                   1
 2  3  4  5  6  7  8
 9 10 11 12 13 14 15
16 17 18 19 20 21 22
23 24 25 26 27 28 29
30 31
```

SEPTEMBER
```
M  T  W  T  F  S  S
       1  2  3  4  5
 6  7  8  9 10 11 12
13 14 15 16 17 18 19
20 21 22 23 24 25 26
27 28 29 30
```

OCTOBER
```
M  T  W  T  F  S  S
             1  2  3
 4  5  6  7  8  9 10
11 12 13 14 15 16 17
18 19 20 21 22 23 24
25 26 27 28 29 30 31
```

NOVEMBER
```
M  T  W  T  F  S  S
 1  2  3  4  5  6  7
 8  9 10 11 12 13 14
15 16 17 18 19 20 21
22 23 24 25 26 27 28
29 30
```

DECEMBER
```
M  T  W  T  F  S  S
       1  2  3  4  5
 6  7  8  9 10 11 12
13 14 15 16 17 18 19
20 21 22 23 24 25 26
27 28 29 30 31
```

2000

JANUARY
```
M  T  W  T  F  S  S
                1  2
 3  4  5  6  7  8  9
10 11 12 13 14 15 16
17 18 19 20 21 22 23
24 25 26 27 28 29 30
31
```

FEBRUARY
```
M  T  W  T  F  S  S
    1  2  3  4  5  6
 7  8  9 10 11 12 13
14 15 16 17 18 19 20
21 22 23 24 25 26 27
28 29
```

MARCH
```
M  T  W  T  F  S  S
          1  2  3  4  5
 6  7  8  9 10 11 12
13 14 15 16 17 18 19
20 21 22 23 24 25 26
27 28 29 30 31
```

APRIL
```
M  T  W  T  F  S  S
                1  2
 3  4  5  6  7  8  9
10 11 12 13 14 15 16
17 18 19 20 21 22 23
24 25 26 27 28 29 30
```

MAY
```
M  T  W  T  F  S  S
 1  2  3  4  5  6  7
 8  9 10 11 12 13 14
15 16 17 18 19 20 21
22 23 24 25 26 27 28
29 30 31
```

JUNE
```
M  T  W  T  F  S  S
          1  2  3  4
 5  6  7  8  9 10 11
12 13 14 15 16 17 18
19 20 21 22 23 24 25
26 27 28 29 30
```

JULY
```
M  T  W  T  F  S  S
                1  2
 3  4  5  6  7  8  9
10 11 12 13 14 15 16
17 18 19 20 21 22 23
24 25 26 27 28 29 30
31
```

AUGUST
```
M  T  W  T  F  S  S
    1  2  3  4  5  6
 7  8  9 10 11 12 13
14 15 16 17 18 19 20
21 22 23 24 25 26 27
28 29 30 31
```

SEPTEMBER
```
M  T  W  T  F  S  S
             1  2  3
 4  5  6  7  8  9 10
11 12 13 14 15 16 17
18 19 20 21 22 23 24
25 26 27 28 29 30
```

OCTOBER
```
M  T  W  T  F  S  S
                   1
 2  3  4  5  6  7  8
 9 10 11 12 13 14 15
16 17 18 19 20 21 22
23 24 25 26 27 28 29
30 31
```

NOVEMBER
```
M  T  W  T  F  S  S
       1  2  3  4  5
 6  7  8  9 10 11 12
13 14 15 16 17 18 19
20 21 22 23 24 25 26
27 28 29 30
```

DECEMBER
```
M  T  W  T  F  S  S
             1  2  3
 4  5  6  7  8  9 10
11 12 13 14 15 16 17
18 19 20 21 22 23 24
25 26 27 28 29 30 31
```

2001

JANUARY
```
M  T  W  T  F  S  S
 1  2  3  4  5  6  7
 8  9 10 11 12 13 14
15 16 17 18 19 20 21
22 23 24 25 26 27 28
29 30 31
```

FEBRUARY
```
M  T  W  T  F  S  S
          1  2  3  4
 5  6  7  8  9 10 11
12 13 14 15 16 17 18
19 20 21 22 23 24 25
26 27 28
```

MARCH
```
M  T  W  T  F  S  S
          1  2  3  4
 5  6  7  8  9 10 11
12 13 14 15 16 17 18
19 20 21 22 23 24 25
26 27 28 29 30 31
```

APRIL
```
M  T  W  T  F  S  S
                   1
 2  3  4  5  6  7  8
 9 10 11 12 13 14 15
16 17 18 19 20 21 22
23 24 25 26 27 28 29
30
```

MAY
```
M  T  W  T  F  S  S
    1  2  3  4  5  6
 7  8  9 10 11 12 13
14 15 16 17 18 19 20
21 22 23 24 25 26 27
28 29 30 31
```

JUNE
```
M  T  W  T  F  S  S
             1  2  3
 4  5  6  7  8  9 10
11 12 13 14 15 16 17
18 19 20 21 22 23 24
25 26 27 28 29 30
```

JULY
```
M  T  W  T  F  S  S
                   1
 2  3  4  5  6  7  8
 9 10 11 12 13 14 15
16 17 18 19 20 21 22
23 24 25 26 27 28 29
30 31
```

AUGUST
```
M  T  W  T  F  S  S
       1  2  3  4  5
 6  7  8  9 10 11 12
13 14 15 16 17 18 19
20 21 22 23 24 25 26
27 28 29 30 31
```

SEPTEMBER
```
M  T  W  T  F  S  S
                1  2
 3  4  5  6  7  8  9
10 11 12 13 14 15 16
17 18 19 20 21 22 23
24 25 26 27 28 29 30
```

OCTOBER
```
M  T  W  T  F  S  S
 1  2  3  4  5  6  7
 8  9 10 11 12 13 14
15 16 17 18 19 20 21
22 23 24 25 26 27 28
29 30 31
```

NOVEMBER
```
M  T  W  T  F  S  S
          1  2  3  4
 5  6  7  8  9 10 11
12 13 14 15 16 17 18
19 20 21 22 23 24 25
26 27 28 29 30
```

DECEMBER
```
M  T  W  T  F  S  S
                1  2
 3  4  5  6  7  8  9
10 11 12 13 14 15 16
17 18 19 20 21 22 23
24 25 26 27 28 29 30
31
```